The Death of Rodriguez

CUBA
IN WAR TIME

BY

RICHARD HARDING DAVIS

ILLUSTRATED BY

FREDERIC REMINGTON

INTRODUCTION TO THE BISON BOOKS EDITION BY

MATTHEW M. OYOS

UNIVERSITY OF NEBRASKA PRESS
LINCOLN AND LONDON

⊗

First Bison Books printing: 2000
Most recent printing indicated by the last digit below:
10   9   8   7   6   5   4   3   2   1

Library of Congress Cataloging-in-Publication Data
Davis, Richard Harding, 1864–1916.
Cuba in war time / by Richard Harding Davis; illustrated by
Frederic Remington; introduction to the Bison Books Edition by
Matthew M. Oyos.
p.   cm.
Originally published: New York: R. H. Russell, 1898.
ISBN 0-8032-6625-1 (pbk.: alk. paper)
1. Davis, Richard Harding, 1864–1916.   2. Cuba—History—
Revolution, 1895–1898—Personal narratives, American.   I. Title.
F1786.D27   2000
972.91′05—dc21
00-034394

This Bison Books edition follows the original in beginning chapter
1 on arabic page 11; no material has been omitted.

INTRODUCTION

Matthew M. Oyos

Richard Harding Davis belonged to an age of titans. At the turn of the twentieth century, Davis dominated popular writing much as Theodore Roosevelt bestrode politics, John D. Rockefeller and J. P. Morgan mastered the economy, and William Randolph Hearst and Joseph Pulitzer forged publishing empires. Unlike those giants, but similar to the titans of Greek lore, Davis languished largely forgotten once less inspiring, more skeptical times arrived. His writing, however, remains a monument to an era when Americans were preparing themselves and their country for a new century. The values, styles, aspirations, and actions of the day may be understood through his work. *Cuba in War Time* paints in vivid strokes the revolutionary turmoil in Cuba in the 1890s and the American outrage that would lead the United States and Spain to battle over the last remnants of the once mighty Spanish empire.

Born into a family of letters, Richard Harding Davis inherited a knack for writing. His mother, Rebecca Harding Davis, had injected stark realism into American fiction in 1861 with her short story "Life in the Iron Mills." Davis's father, Clarke, was a lawyer who became one of Philadelphia's leading journalists and newspaper publishers. Richard Harding Davis combined the literary talents and tastes of his parents. He also went many steps beyond them. Davis was prolific, producing an enormous quantity of books, serialized stories, and newspaper reports. He fashioned himself as a writer-observer, a role that encompassed journalism, fiction and nonfiction writing, and even drama. But most important, in this field in which Rebecca and Clarke Davis had established reputations chiefly among eastern intellectuals and literary lights, their son became one

of America's most recognized figures, nationally and interna-
tionally, during the two decades that bracketed the turn of the
twentieth century.

Richard Harding Davis won his reputation on the strength
of works such as *Cuba in War Time*. He was, in short, the
American Rudyard Kipling. Similarly to the British author, he
assured his audiences that strenuous living, courage, and bold-
ness were alive in an age of rapid industrialization and urban-
ization. As in Kipling's works, set primarily in India, the main
arena for action in Davis's work lay overseas, but in Latin
America. Davis, like Kipling, made an adventurous life in an
exotic setting not only attractive but a duty: the advanced, En-
glish-speaking peoples were to bring the best of their civilization to benighted peoples and keep themselves morally superior and physically robust in the process. Davis, moreover, at-
tempted to live the life that he described. A handsome, dash-
ing figure, he traveled throughout the United States and then
the world in search of remarkable stories. He first captured
readers' imaginations with a character named Cortlandt Van
Bibber, a gentleman hero who gallantly saved people in distress and dispensed justice to wrongdoers. Van Bibber was something of a self-portrait, but Davis found he could surpass his
creation with tales of his own travels and adventures. The Cuban war for independence suited him perfectly.

Cuba erupted in revolt against Spanish rule in 1895. The
conflict followed a previously unsuccessful effort at independence, the "Ten Years War" of 1868–78. Nationalists such as
José Martí refused to accept that defeat and inspired the new
insurrection. Cuba was soon aflame in a savage conflict, and
Americans grew fascinated with events on the nearby island.
Cuba's struggle against a colonial ruler struck a familiar chord
with Americans, who were also making large investments in
the island's economy. The Cuban-Spanish war, in fact, increas-
ingly represented an opportunity for the newly industrialized
United States to flex its muscles and exercise influence. Pub-
lisher William Randolph Hearst of the *New York Journal* recognized a compelling story and decided that Richard Harding

Davis, America's most famous writer of true adventure, was
the perfect reporter for the job. Along with Davis, Hearst re-
cruited the artist Frederic Remington to insure that the result-
ing story had a graphic punch.

The muscular prose captured in *Cuba in War Time* could
have fired American imaginations even without Remington's
distinctive sketches. Davis supplied the quintessential real-life
drama. Based on the news dispatches sent to the *Journal, Cuba
in Wartime* is part travelogue, part morality tale, part call-to-
arms, and part action story. Davis conveyed a vibrant, three-
dimensional rendering of Cuba so that his readers, who lived
just before the age of motion picture theaters, could feel the
texture of life on the island. The Cuban sky, for example,
emerges "as great expanses of blue, and in the early morning
and before sunset, they are lighted with wonderful clouds of
pink and saffron, as brilliant and as unreal as the fairy's grotto
in a pantomime." Davis's portrayals of people are even more
compelling, especially in his classic account of the Spanish
execution of a Cuban insurgent. In the chapter "The Death of
Rodriguez," Adolfo Rodriguez has the "handsome, gentle face
of the peasant type, a light, pointed beard, great wistful eyes
and a mass of curly black hair." The drama of the moment
stems from the young man's nonchalance in smoking a cigarette before his death and a delay in the execution owing to an
officer's incompetence. Davis writes as if the reader were ob-
serving beside him, for ultimately he did not want simply to
leave an impression but to inspire the reader to action.

Davis makes no pretense at objectivity in this work. He began his journey to Cuba as a noninterventionist, but his sym-
pathies soon shifted. He leaves no doubt that he sides with the
Cuban *insurrectos* against the Spanish authorities. He indulges,
in fact, in disparaging the Spaniards with slurs designed to
incite his reading public. Davis describes the Cubans as brave
and heroic, but he portrays the Spaniards as murderers who
behave "worse than savage animals" and fall below the level
of cannibals. Davis intends this tale of good versus evil to arouse
American indignation and provoke intervention. In this man-

ner, *Cuba in War Time* attains importance as a historical document. Pro-war "jingoes" used many of the stories contained in the text to justify war with Spain. The book thus revives for the reader the imperialistic spirit of America at the turn of the twentieth century, a time when people viewed great national issues in absolute terms and citizens exuded confidence in a broader political, economic, and cultural destiny for their country. It was also a time when politicians and intellectuals applied Darwin's theories of evolution to nations, with some arguing that wars affirmed masculinity and insured continued national fitness in a world of great powers.

Davis's account is especially helpful for recapturing images that were indelibly etched into the consciousness of the Spanish-American War generation. He introduced many Americans to the shockingly desperate conditions in the Reconcentration Camps, which the Spaniards designed to keep the civilian population from supporting the Cuban guerrillas. Filth, disease, and death ruled the camps and illustrated the callousness of Spanish rule. Davis also managed to outrage Victorian sensibilities with his description of the intimate search of three Cuban women. Spanish authorities suspected the women of helping the rebels and ordered them into exile. Before allowing them to proceed to the United States, the Spaniards detained and searched them. The story of the women quickly became fodder for the "yellow press," sensationalistic newspapers of which Hearst's *Journal* was a prime example. Sales drove these newspapers more than accuracy, and the particular journalistic liberties taken with Davis's story of the Cuban women contributed mightily to the emotional outcry against Spain. In *Cuba in Wartime*, Davis states that a female official conducted the search, but that was not the story the American public initially received. Davis's first dispatch about the incident failed to mention the female official, so William Randolph Hearst commissioned a drawing that showed a naked girl being searched by male officers. The portrayal fanned interventionist flames and sold thousands of newspapers. Stung by Hearst's journalistic license, an angry Davis corrected the record, stressing repeatedly and carefully, as he does in the book, the true nature of the events. He did not, however, reduce the impact of Hearst's story and its place in the coming of the war with Spain. Nor did he particularly want to, for Davis was wedded firmly to American intervention by this point.

Although he could not have realized it at the time, Davis previewed some of the toughest, most trying wars in the twentieth century. The Cuban war was messy, politically complex, and hard to resolve. It was a people's war, not a struggle where standing armies met each other on the open field of battle. Davis describes a guerrilla conflict in which the combatants were not easily detected and civilians were caught between competing forces. Frustrations mounted on both sides, and atrocities abounded during the protracted fighting. In its broadest outlines, in fact, the conflict contains foreshadowing haunting to the modern reader. The Reconcentration Camps resemble too closely, in name and conditions, the death camps of World War II. Moreover, the camps proved about as helpful to the Spanish cause as the fortified "Strategic Hamlets" of the Vietnam War did for containing communist insurgency. Finally, the Spaniards' ability to govern the cities but not the countryside has an almost universal ring to it, as do their futile attempts to create physical barriers to guerrilla movement.

Students of the twentieth century may wonder why Davis's generation of readers did not receive this book as a cautionary tale about the grim side of war. Although *Cuba in War Time* relays harsh realities, Davis represents the Cuban-Spanish conflict primarily as a grand test of the human spirit. For him, war is a crucible in which people reveal either their noblest or their basest instincts. His Kiplingesque sense of superiority also suggests a belief that Americans would not be subject to the same kind of grinding contest that the impoverished Cubans and the declining Spaniards found themselves trapped into fighting. Davis implies, instead, that Americans could impose their own style of war at will. Only hard experience in the twentieth century would erode such arrogance.

The United States, of course, got its war in Cuba, and Rich-

ard Harding Davis was there in 1898 to cover it. He did not
find a splendid war; instead, he witnessed the travail of an
army that had not fought a major war in more than thirty years.
Davis did not spare the top commanders of the Cuban expedition in *The Cuban and Porto Rican Campaigns*, his sequel to
Cuba in War Time, but he still found plenty of glory to report
in Cuba. Shrewdly, he attached himself to the First United States
Volunteer Cavalry Regiment, that amalgam of eastern elites
and western cowboys known as the Rough Riders. Led by Col.
Leonard Wood and Lt. Col. Theodore Roosevelt, the Rough
Riders embodied the best of the American fighting spirit for
Davis. The unit boasted eastern men of action who were cut
from the same cloth as Davis himself and westerners who embodied the hardihood and the rambunctiousness of the fron-
tier. Davis dramatized the Rough Riders' clash with Spanish
forces at Las Guásimas, and he detailed Roosevelt's assault on
the San Juan hills outside Santiago de Cuba. In so doing, he
enshrined Theodore Roosevelt in American popular culture and
helped clear a path for the Rough Rider that led directly from
the San Juan hills to the White House.

Roosevelt's star was not the only one that sparkled as a result of news reports. Davis's own image shone brightly, for he
was at the height of his powers and fame at the time. The national and international recognition accorded Davis heralded
the continuing and rapid transformation of journalism at the
turn of the twentieth century. Already wire services meant the
speedy collection and dissemination of news, and with growing urban markets newspapers were becoming big business.
The ascent of Davis's persona signaled another trend: the rise
of the journalist as celebrity and entertainer. The very mention
of the name Richard Harding Davis conjured up expectations
of lively, engrossing stories. That association, in turn, sold books
and newspapers. William Randolph Hearst had recognized as
much when he dispatched Davis to Cuba in 1897, and so did
Davis. Davis, in fact, acknowledged the power of his name
and loved the attention he received. He played the role of re-
porter-celebrity to the hilt, from his immaculate dress to his

efforts to feed his public a regular stream of stories, books, reports, and dramas. To be sure, Davis had his critics. He was frequently derided as superficial; however, as long as his name remained recognized and sales were strong, he could ignore such criticism with serene confidence.

Richard Harding Davis was fortunate, to some extent, that he did not live beyond World War I. He died in 1916 at the age of fifty-two while working on an account of the French at war. Davis had sensed the desolation spawned by the conflict, but he would have been lost among the generation of writers that followed the war. He wrote to entertain, and his writing had purpose and moral conviction to it. The disillusionment of the postwar writers would have troubled and mystified him. He had written for a generation confident of progress and a higher purpose, but such self-assurance evaporated in the bloodbath that sapped western civilization from 1914 to 1918. Ironically, Davis's rousing, romanticized tomes had helped make possible the very war that ultimately ended the widespread acceptance of such works.

The literary and cultural revolution wrought by World War I—in addition to the political, social, and economic upheavals—makes the reading of books such as *Cuba in War Time* all the more important. This volume provides a portal to a lost world. Through it, the reader recaptures the feeling of a bygone age. Davis's bold prose recalls a time when the world was often, for good or ill, viewed in black and white terms. His writing also returns the reader to an era when Americans felt they were coming of age as a people and were eager to assert a larger destiny for their nation. A sense of mission emerges as Americans were about to define a new—and often troubled—relationship with the people of Cuba. For the latter-day reader, *Cuba in War Time* is full of portent for the events of the twentieth century, but above all it remains a fascinating and enduring story of human drama.

Contents

Illustrations

NOTE

These illustrations were made by Mr. Frederic Remington, from personal observation while in Cuba, and from photographs, and descriptions furnished by eye-witnesses.

Author's Note

AFTER my return from Cuba many people asked me questions concerning the situation there, and I noticed that they generally asked the same questions. This book has been published with the idea of answering those questions as fully as is possible for me to do after a journey through the island, during which I traveled in four of the six provinces, visiting towns, seaports, plantations and military camps, and stopping for several days in all of the chief cities of Cuba, with the exception of Santiago and Pinar del Rio.

Part of this book was published originally in the form of letters from Cuba to the *New York Journal* and in the newspapers of a syndicate arranged by the *Journal*; the remainder, which was suggested by the questions asked on my return, was written in this country, and appears here for the first time.

RICHARD HARDING DAVIS.

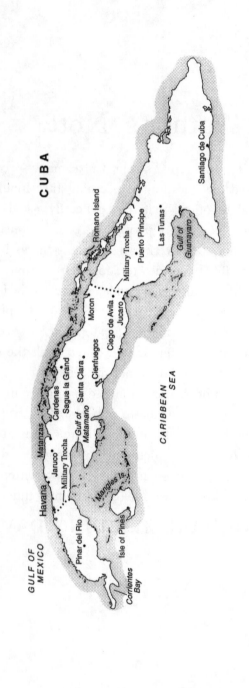

Cuba in War Time

WHEN the revolution broke out in Cuba two years ago, the Spaniards at once began to build tiny forts, and continued to add to these and improve those already built, until now the whole island, which is eight hundred miles long and averages eighty miles in width, is studded as thickly with these little forts as is the sole of a brogan with iron nails. It is necessary to keep the fact of the existence of these forts in mind in order to understand the situation in Cuba at the present time, as they illustrate the Spanish plan of campaign, and explain why the war has dragged on for so long, and why it may continue indefinitely.

The last revolution was organized by the aristocrats; the present one is a revolution of the *pueblco*, and, while the principal Cuban families are again among the leaders, with them now are the representatives of the "plain people," and the cause is now a common cause in working for the success of which all classes of Cubans are desperately in earnest.

The outbreak of this revolution was hastened by an offer from Spain to make certain reforms in the internal government of the island. The old revolutionary leaders, fearing that the promise of these reforms might satisfy the Cubans, and that they would cease to hope for complete independence, started the revolt, and asked all loyal Cubans not to accept the so-called reforms when, by fighting, they might obtain their freedom. Another cause which precipitated the revolution was the financial depression which existed all over the island in 1894, and the closing of the sugar mills in consequence. Owing to the lack of money with which to pay the laborers, the grinding of the sugar cane ceased, and the men were turned off by the hundreds, and, for want of something better to do, joined the insurgents. Some planters believe that had Spain loaned them sufficient money with which to continue grinding, the men would have remained on the *centrals*, as the machine shops and residence of a sugar plantation are called, and that so few would have gone into the field against Spain that the insurrection could have been put down before it had gained headway. An advance to the sugar planters of five millions of dollars then, so they say, would have saved Spain the outlay of many hundreds of millions spent later in supporting an army

in the field. That may or may not be true, and it
is not important now, for Spain did not attack the
insurgents in that way, but began hastily to build
forts. These forts now stretch all over the island,
some in straight lines, some in circles, and some
zig-zagging from hill-top to hill-top, some within
a quarter of a mile of the next, and others so near
that the sentries can toss a cartridge from one to
the other.

The island is divided into two great military
camps, one situated within the forts, and the other
scattered over the fields and mountains outside
of them. The Spaniards have absolute control
over everything within the fortified places; that is,
in all cities, towns, seaports, and along the lines of
the railroad; the insurgents are in possession of all
the rest. They are not in fixed possession, but they
have control much as a mad bull may be said to
have control of a ten-acre lot when he goes on the
rampage. Some farmer may hold a legal right to
the ten-acre lot, through title deeds or in the shape
of a mortgage, and the bull may occupy but one
part of it at a time, but he has possession, which is
better than the law.

It is difficult to imagine a line drawn so closely,
not about one city or town, but around every city
and town in Cuba, that no one can pass the line

from either the outside or the inside.   The Spaniards, however, have succeeded in effecting and
maintaining a blockade of that kind.   They have
placed forts next to the rows of houses or huts on
the outskirts of each town, within a hundred yards
of one another, and outside of this circle is another
circle, and beyond that, on every high piece of
ground, are still more of these little square forts,
which are not much larger than the signal stations
along the lines of our railroads and not unlike them
in appearance.   No one can cross the line of the
forts without a pass, nor enter from the country beyond them without an order showing from
what place he comes, at what time he left that place,
and that he had permission from the commandante
to leave it. A stranger in any city in Cuba to-day is
virtually in a prison, and is as isolated from the rest
of the world as though he were on a desert island or
a floating ship of war. When he wishes to depart he
is free to do so, but he cannot leave on foot nor on
horseback.   He must make his departure on a
railroad train, of which seldom more than two
leave any town in twenty-four hours, one going
east and the other west.   From Havana a number
of trains depart daily in different directions, but
once outside of Havana, there is only one train
back to it again,   When on the cars you are still in

A Spanish Soldier

the presence and under the care of Spanish soldiers, and the progress of the train is closely
guarded. A pilot engine precedes it at a distance
of one hundred yards to test the rails and pick up
dynamite bombs, and in front of it is a car covered
with armor plate, with slits in the sides like those
in a letter box, through which the soldiers may fire.
There are generally from twenty to fifty soldiers in
each armored car. Back of the armored car is a flat
car loaded with ties, girders and rails, which are
used to repair bridges or those portions of the track
that may have been blown up by the insurgents.
Wherever a track crosses a bridge there are two
forts, one at each end of the bridge, and also at almost every cross-road. When the train passes one
of these forts, two soldiers appear in the door and
stand at salute to show, probably, that they are
awake, and at every station there are two or
more forts, while the stations themselves are usually
protected by ramparts of ties and steel rails. There
is no situation where it is so distinctly evident that
those who are not with you are against you, for you
are either inside of one circle of forts or passing
under guard by rail to another circle, or you are with
the insurgents. There is no alternative. If you walk
fifty yards away from the circle you are, in the eyes
of the Spaniards, as much in "the field" as though

you were two hundred miles away on the mountains.

The lines are so closely drawn that when you consider the tremendous amount of time and labor expended in keeping up this blockade, you must admire the Spaniards for doing it so well, but you would admire them more, if, instead of stopping content with that they went further and invaded the field. The forts are an excellent precaution; they prevent sympathizers from joining the insurgents and from sending them food, arms, medicine or messages. But the next step, after blockading the cities, would appear to be to follow the insurgents into the field and give them battle. This the Spaniards do not seem to consider important, nor wish to do. Flying columns of regular troops and **guerrillas are sent out daily, but they always return each evening within the circle of forts. If they** meet a band of insurgents they give battle readily enough, but they never pursue the enemy, and, instead of camping on the ground and following him up the next morning, they retreat as soon as the battle is over, to the town where they are stationed. When occasionally objection is made to this by a superior officer, they give as an explanation that they were afraid of being led into an ambush, and that as an officer's first consideration must be for his men, they decided that it was wiser not to follow the enemy into what might prove a death-trap; or the officers say they could not abandon their wounded while they pursued the rebels. Sometimes a force of one thousand men will return with three men wounded, and will offer their condition as an excuse for having failed to follow the enemy.

About five years ago troops of United States cavalry were sent into the chapparal on the border of Mexico and Texas to drive the Garcia revolutionists back into their own country. One troop, G, Third Cavalry, was ordered out for seven days' service, but when I joined the troop later as a correspondent, it had been in the field for three months, sleeping the entire time under canvas, and carrying all its impedimenta with it on pack mules. It had seldom, if ever, been near a town, and the men wore the same clothes, or what was left of them, with which they had started for a week's campaign. Had the Spaniards followed such a plan of attack as that when the revolution began, instead of building mud forts and devastating the country, they might not only have suppressed the revolution, but the country would have been of some value when the war ended. As it is to-day, it will take ten years or more to bring it back to a condition of productiveness.

The wholesale devastation of the island was an idea of General Weyler's. If the captain of a vessel, in order to put down a mutiny on board, scuttled the ship and sent everybody to the bottom, his plan of action would be as successful as General Weyler's has proved to be. After he had obtained complete control of the cities he decided to lay waste the country and starve the revolutionists into submission. So he ordered all pacificos, as the non-belligerents are called, into the towns and burned their houses, and issued orders to have all fields where potatoes or corn were planted dug up and these food products destroyed.

These pacificos are now gathered inside of a dead line, drawn one hundred and fifty yards around the towns, or wherever there is a fort. Some of them have settled around the forts that guard a bridge, others around the forts that guard a sugar plantation; wherever there are forts there are pacificos.

In a word, the situation in Cuba is something like this: The Spaniards hold the towns, from which their troops daily make predatory raids, invariably returning in time for dinner at night. Around each town is a circle of pacificos doing no work, and for the most part starving and diseased, and outside, in the plains and mountains, are the insurgents. No one knows just where any one band of them is to-

Guerillas With Captured Pacificos

day, or where it may be to-morrow. Sometimes they come up to the very walls of the fort, lasso a bunch of cattle and ride off again, and the next morning their presence may be detected ten miles away, where they are setting fire to a cane field or a sugar plantation.

This is the situation, so far as the inhabitants are concerned. The physical appearance of the country since the war began has changed greatly. In the days of peace Cuba was one of the most beautiful islands in the tropics, perhaps in the world. Its skies hang low and are brilliantly beautiful, with great expanses of blue, and in the early morning and before sunset, they are lighted with wonderful clouds of pink and saffron, as brilliant and as unreal as the fairy's grotto in a pantomime. There are great wind-swept prairies of high grass or tall sugar cane, and on the sea coast mountains of a light green, like the green of corroded copper, changing to a darker shade near the base, where they are covered with forests of palms.

Throughout the extent of the island run many little streams, sometimes between high banks of rock, covered with moss and magnificent fern, with great pools of clear, deep water at the base of high waterfalls, and in those places where the stream cuts its way through the level plains double rows of the royal palm mark its course. The royal palm is the characteristic feature of the landscape in Cuba. It is the most beautiful of all palms, and possibly the most beautiful of all trees. The cocoanut palm, as one sees it in Egypt, picturesque as it is, has a pathetic resemblance to a shabby feather duster, and its trunk bends and twists as though it had not the strength to push its way through the air, and to hold itself erect. But the royal palm shoots up boldly from the earth with the grace and symmetry of a marble pillar or the white mast of a great ship. Its trunk swells in the centre and grows smaller again at the top, where it is hidden by great bunches of green plumes, like monstrous ostrich feathers that wave and bow and bend in the breeze as do the plumes on the head of a beautiful woman. Standing isolated in an open plain or in ranks in a forest of palms, this tree is always beautiful, noble and full of meaning. It makes you forget the ugly iron chimneys of the *centrals*, and it is the first and the last feature that appeals to the visitor in Cuba.

But since the revolution came to Cuba the beauty of the landscape is blotted with the grim and pitiable signs of war. The sugar cane has turned to a dirty brown where the fire has passed through it, the *centrals* are black ruins, and the adobe houses and the railroad stations are roofless, and their broken windows stare pathetically at you like blind eyes. War cannot alter the sunshine, but the smoke from the burning huts and the blazing corn fields seems all the more sad and terrible when it rises into such an atmosphere, and against so soft and beautiful a sky.

People frequently ask how far the destruction of property in Cuba is apparent. · It is so far apparent that the smoke of burning buildings is seldom absent from the landscape. If you stand on an elevation it is possible to see from ten to twenty blazing houses, and the smoke from the cane fields creeping across the plain or rising slowly to meet the sky. Sometimes the train passes for hours through burning districts, and the heat from the fields along the track is so intense that it is impossible to keep the windows up, and whenever the door is opened sparks and cinders sweep into the car. One morning, just this side of Jovellanos, all the sugar cane on the right side of the track was wrapped in white smoke for miles so that nothing could be distinguished from that side of the car, and we seemed to be moving through the white steam of a Russian bath.

The Spaniards are no more to blame for this than are the insurgents; each destroy property and burn the cane. When an insurgent column finds a field planted with potatoes, it takes as much of the crop as it can carry away and chops up the remainder with machetes, to prevent it from falling into the hands of the Spaniards. If the Spaniards pass first, they act in exactly the same way.

Cane is not completely destroyed if it is burned, for if it is at once cut down just above the roots, it will grow again. When peace is declared it will not be the soil that will be found wanting, nor the sun. It will be the lack of money and the loss of credit that will keep the sugar planters from sowing and grinding. And the loss of machinery in the *centrals*, which is worth in single instances hundreds of thousands of dollars, and in the aggregate many millions, cannot be replaced by men, who, even when their machinery was intact, were on the brink of ruin.

Unless the United States government interferes on account of some one of its citizens in Cuba, and war is declared with Spain, there is no saying how long the present revolution may continue. For the Spaniards themselves are acting in a way which makes many people suspect that they are not making an effort to bring it to an end. The sincerity of the Spaniards in Spain is beyond question; the personal sacrifices they made in taking up the loans

A Spanish Officer

issued by the government are proof of their loyalty. But the Spaniards in Cuba are acting for their own interests. Many of the planters in order to save their fields and *centrals* from destruction, are unquestionably aiding the insurgents in secret, and though they shout "Viva España" in the cities, they pay out cartridges and money at the back door of their plantations.

It was because Weyler suspected that they were playing this double game that he issued secret orders that there should be no more grinding. For he knew that the same men who bribed him to allow them to grind would also pay blackmail to the insurgents for a like permission. He did not dare openly to forbid the grinding, but he instructed his officers in the field to visit those places where grinding was in progress and to stop it by some indirect means, such as by declaring that the laborers employed were suspects, or by seizing all the draught oxen ostensibly for the use of his army, or by insisting that the men employed must show a fresh permit to work every day, which could only be issued to them by some commandante stationed not less than ten miles distant from the plantation on which they were employed.

And the Spanish officers, as well as the planters— the very men to whom Spain looks to end the rebel-

lion—are chief among those who are keeping it
alive.   The reasons for their doing so are obvious;
they receive double pay while they are on foreign
service, whether they are fighting or not, promo-
tion comes twice as quickly as in time of peace, and
orders and crosses are distributed by the gross.
They are also able to make small fortunes out of
forced loans from planters and suspects, and they
undoubtedly hold back for themselves a great part
of the pay of the men.   A certain class of Spanish
officer has a strange sense of honor.   He does
not consider that robbing his government by falsi-
fying his accounts, or by making incorrect returns
of his expenses, is disloyal or unpatriotic. He holds
such an act as lightly as many people do smuggling
cigars through their own custom house, or robbing a
corporation of a railroad fare.   He might be perfectly willing to die for his country, but should he
be permitted to live he will not hesitate to rob her.

A lieutenant, for instance, will take twenty men
out for their daily walk through the surrounding
country and after burning a few huts and butcher-
ing a pacifico or two, will come back in time for
dinner and charge his captain for rations for fifty
men and for three thousand cartridges "expended
in service."   The captain visés his report, and the
two share the profits.   Or they turn the money

over to the colonel, who recommends them for red
enamelled crosses for "bravery on the field." The
only store in Matanzas that was doing a brisk trade
when I was there was a jewelry shop, where they
had sold more diamonds and watches to the Spanish officers since the revolution broke out than they
had ever been able to dispose of before to all the
rich men in the city. The legitimate pay of the
highest ranking officer is barely enough to buy red
wine for his dinner, certainly not enough to pay for
champagne and diamonds; so it is not unfair to suppose that the rebellion is a profitable experience for
the officers, and they have no intention of losing
the golden eggs.

And the insurgents on the other side are equally
determined to continue the conflict. From every
point of view this is all that is left for them to do.
They know by terrible experience how little of
mercy or even of justice they may expect from
the enemy, and, patriotism or the love of independence aside, it is better for them to die in the
field than to risk the other alternative; a lin-
gering life in an African penal settlement or the
fusillade against the east wall of Cabañas prison. In
an island with a soil so rich and productive as is
that of Cuba there will always be roots and fruits
for the insurgents to live upon, and with the cattle

that they have hidden away in the laurel or on the mountains they can keep their troops in rations for an indefinite period. What they most need now are cartridges and rifles. Of men they have already more than they can arm.

People in the United States frequently express impatience at the small amount of fighting which takes place in this struggle for liberty, and it is true that the lists of killed show that the death rate in battle is inconsiderable. Indeed, when compared with the number of men and women who die daily of small-pox and fever and those who are butchered on the plantations, the proportion of killed in battle is probably about one to fifteen.

I have no statistics to prove these figures, but, judging from the hospital reports and from what the consuls tell of the many murders of pacificos, I judge that that proportion would be rather under than above the truth. George Bronson Rae, the *Herald* correspondent, who was for nine months with Maceo and Gomez, and who saw eighty fights and was twice wounded, told me that the largest number of insurgents he had seen killed in one battle was thirteen.

Another correspondent said that a Spanish officer had told him that he had killed forty insurgents out of four hundred who had attacked his column.

Insurgents Firing on a Spanish Fort

"One Shot for a Hundred"

"But how do you know you killed that many?" the correspondent asked. "You say you were never nearer than half a mile to them, and that you fell back into the town as soon as they ceased firing."

"Ah, but I counted the cartridges my men had used," the officer replied. "I found they had expended four hundred. By allowing ten bullets to each man killed, I was able to learn that we had killed forty men."

These stories show how little reason there is to speak of these skirmishes as battles, and it also throws some light on the Spaniard's idea of his own marksmanship. As a plain statement of fact, and without any exaggeration, one of the chief reasons why half the insurgents in Cuba are not dead to-day is because the Spanish soldiers cannot shoot well enough to hit them. The Mauser rifle, which is used by all the Spanish soldiers, with the exception of the Guardia Civile, is a most excellent weapon for those who like clean, gentlemanly warfare, in which the object is to wound or to kill outright, and not to "shock" the enemy nor to tear his flesh in pieces. The weapon has hardly any trajectory up to one thousand yards, but, in spite of its precision, it is as useless in the hands of a guerrilla or the average Spanish soldier as a bow and arrow would be. The fact that when the Spaniards say "within gun fire of the forts" they mean within one hundred and fifty yards of them shows how they estimate their own skill. Major Grover Flint, the *Journal* correspondent, told me of a fight that he witnessed in which the Spaniards fired two thousand rounds at forty insurgents only two hundred yards away, and only succeeded in wounding three of them. Sylvester Scovel once explained this bad marksmanship to me by pointing out that to shift the cartridge in a Mauser, it is necessary to hold the rifle at an almost perpendicular angle, and close up under the shoulder. After the fresh cartridge has gone home the temptation to bring the butt to the shoulder before the barrel is level is too great for the Spanish Tommy, and, in his excitement, he fires most of his ammunition in the air over the heads of the enemy. He also fires so recklessly and rapidly that his gun often becomes too hot for him to handle it properly, and it is not an unusual sight to see him rest the butt on the ground and pull the trigger while the gun is in that position.

On the whole, the Spanish soldiers during this war in Cuba have contributed little to the information of those who are interested in military science. The tactics which the officers follow are those which were found effective at the battle of Water-

loo, and in the Peninsular campaign. When attacked from an ambush a Spanish column forms at
once into a hollow square, with the cavalry in the
centre, and the firing is done in platoons. They
know nothing of "open order," or of firing in skir-
mish line. If the Cubans were only a little better
marksmen than their enemies they should, with
such a target as a square furnishes them, kill about
ten men where they now wound one.

With the war conducted under the conditions
described here, there does not seem to be much
promise of its coming to any immediate end unless
some power will interfere. The Spaniards will
probably continue to remain inside their forts, and
the officers will continue to pay themselves well out
of the rebellion.

And, on the other hand, the insurgents who
call themselves rich when they have three cartridges, as opposed to the one hundred and fifty cartridges that every Spanish soldier carries, will probably very wisely continue to refuse to force the
issue in any one battle.

The Fate of the Pacificos

Fire and Sword in Cuba

The Fate of the Pacificos

As is already well known in the United States, General Weyler issued an order some months ago commanding the country people living in the provinces of Pinar del Rio, Havana and Matanzas to betake themselves with their belongings to the fortified towns. His object in doing this was to prevent the pacificos from giving help to the insurgents, and from sheltering them and the wounded in their huts. So flying columns of guerrillas and Spanish soldiers were sent to burn these huts, and to drive the inhabitants into the suburbs of the cities. When I arrived in Cuba sufficient time had passed for me to note the effects of this order, and to study the results as they are to be found in the provinces of Havana, Matanzas and Santa Clara, the order having been extended to embrace the latter province.

It looked then as though General Weyler was reaping what he had sown, and was face to face with a problem of his own creating. As far as a visitor could judge, the results of this famous order seemed to furnish a better argument to those who think the United States should interfere in behalf of Cuba, than did the fact that men were being killed there, and that both sides were devastating the island and wrecking property worth millions of dollars.

The order, apart from being unprecedented in warfare, proved an exceedingly short-sighted one, and acted almost immediately after the manner of a boomerang. The able-bodied men of each family who had remained loyal or at least neutral, so long as they were permitted to live undisturbed on their few acres, were not content to exist on the charity of a city, and they swarmed over to the insurgent ranks by the hundreds, and it was only the old and infirm and the women and children who went into the towns, where they at once became a burden on the Spanish residents, who were already distressed by the lack of trade and the high prices asked for food.

The order failed also in its original object of embarrassing the insurgents, for they are used to living out of doors and to finding food for themselves, and the destruction of the huts where they had been made welcome was not a great loss to men who, in a few minutes, with the aid of a machete, can construct a shelter from a palm tree.

So the order failed to distress those against whom it was aimed, but brought swift and terrible suffering to those who were and are absolutely innocent of any intent against the government, as well as to the adherents of the government.

It is easy to imagine what happened when hundreds of people, in some towns thousands, were herded together on the bare ground, with no food, with no knowledge of sanitation, with no covering for their heads but palm leaves, with no privacy for the women and young girls, with no thought but as to how they could live until to-morrow.

It is true that in the country, also, these people had no covering for their huts but palm leaves, but those huts were made stoutly to endure. When a man built one of them he was building his home, not a shelter tent, and they were placed well apart from one another, with the free air of the plain or mountain blowing about them, with room for the sun to beat down and drink up the impurities, and with patches of green things growing in rows over the few acres. I have seen them like that all over Cuba, and I am sure that no disease could have sprung from houses built so admirably to admit the sun and the air.

I have also seen them, I might add in parenthe-
sis, rising in sluggish columns of black smoke
against the sky, hundreds of them, while those who
had lived in them for years stood huddled together
at a distance, watching the flames run over the dry
rafters of their homes, roaring and crackling with
delight, like something human or inhuman, and
marring the beautiful sunlit landscape with great
blotches of red flames.

The huts in which these people live at present
lean one against the other, and there are no broad
roads nor green tobacco patches to separate one
from another. There are, on the contrary, only
narrow paths, two feet wide, where dogs and
cattle and human beings tramp over daily growing
heaps of refuse and garbage and filth, and where
malaria rises at night in a white winding sheet of
poisonous mist.

The condition of these people differs in degree;
some are living the life of gypsies, others are as destitute as so many shipwrecked emigrants, and still
others find it difficult to hold up their heads and
breathe.

In Jaruco, in the Havana province, a town of
only two thousand inhabitants, the deaths from
small-pox averaged seven a day for the month of
December, and while Frederic Remington and I

A Spanish Guerrilla

were there, six victims of small-pox were carried
past us up the hill to the burying ground in the
space of twelve hours. There were Spanish soldiers as well as pacificos among these, for the
Spanish officers either know or care nothing about
the health of their men.

There is no attempt made to police these military
camps, and in Jaruco the filth covered the streets
and the plaza ankle-deep, and even filled the cor-
ners of the church which had been turned into a
fort, and had hammocks swung from the altars.
The huts of the pacificos, with from four to six people in each, were jammed together in rows a quarter of a mile long, within ten feet of the cavalry
barracks, where sixty men and horses had lived for
a month. Next to the stables were the barracks. No
one was vaccinated, no one was clean, and all of
them were living on half rations.

Jaruco was a little worse than the other towns,
but I found that the condition of the people is about
the same everywhere. Around every town and
even around the forts outside of the towns, you will
see from one hundred to five hundred of these palm
huts, with the people crouched about them, covered
with rags, starving, with no chance to obtain work.

In the city of Matanzas the huts have been built
upon a hill, and so far neither small-pox nor yellow

fever has made headway there; but there is nothing
for these people to eat, either, and while I was there
three babies died from plain, old-fashioned starvation and no other cause.

The government's report for the year just ended
gives the number of deaths in three hospitals of
Matanzas as three hundred and eighty for the year,
which is an average of a little over one death a day.
As a matter of fact, in the military hospital alone the
soldiers during several months of last year died at
the rate of sixteen a day.   It seems hard that Spain
should hold Cuba at such a sacrifice of her own
people.

In Cardenas, one of the principal seaport towns
of the island, I found the pacificos lodged in huts at
the back of the town and also in abandoned
warehouses along the water front.   The condition
of these latter was so pitiable that it is difficult to
describe it correctly and hope to be believed.

The warehouses are built on wooden posts
about fifty feet from the water's edge.   They were
originally nearly as large in extent as Madison
Square Garden, but the half of the roof of one has
fallen in, carrying the flooring with it, and the
adobe walls and one side of the sloping roof and the
high wooden piles on which half of the floor once
rested are all that remain.

Some time ago an unusually high tide swept in under one of these warehouses and left a pool of water a hundred yards long and as many wide, around the wooden posts, and it has remained there undisturbed. This pool is now covered a half-inch thick with green slime, colored blue and yellow, and with a damp fungus spread over the wooden posts and up the sides of the walls.

Over this sewage are now living three hundred women and children and a few men. The floor beneath them has rotted away, and the planks have broken and fallen into the pool, leaving big gaps, through which rise day and night deadly stenches and poisonous exhalations from the pool below.

The people above it are not ignorant of their situation. They know that they are living over a death-trap, but there is no other place for them. Bands of guerrillas and flying columns have driven them in like sheep to this city, and, with no money and no chance to obtain work, they have taken shelter in the only place that is left open to them.

With planks and blankets and bits of old sheet iron they have, for the sake of decency, put up barriers across these abandoned warehouses, and there they are now sitting on the floor or stretched on heaps of rags, gaunt and hollow-eyed. Outside, in the angles of the fallen walls, and among the refuse of the warehouses, they have built fireplaces, and, with the few pots and kettles they use in common, they cook what food the children can find or beg.

One gentleman of Cardenas told me that a hundred of these people called at his house every day for a bit of food.

Old negroes and little white children, some of them as beautiful, in spite of their rags, as any children I ever saw, act as providers for this hapless colony. They beg the food and gather the sticks and do the cooking. Inside the old women and young mothers sit on the rotten planks listless and silent, staring ahead of them at nothing.

I saw the survivors of the Johnstown flood when the horror of that disaster was still plainly written in their eyes, but destitute as they were of home and food and clothing, they were in better plight than those fever-stricken, starving pacificos, who have sinned in no way, who have given no aid to the rebels, and whose only crime is that they lived in the country instead of in the town. They are now to suffer because General Weyler, finding that he cannot hold the country as he can the towns, lays it waste and treats those who lived there with less consideration than the Sultan of Morocco shows to the murderers in his jail at Tangier. Had these people been guilty of the most unnatural crimes,

Murdering the Cuban Wounded

their punishment could not have been more severe nor their end more certain.

I found the hospital for this colony behind three blankets which had been hung across a corner of the warehouse. A young woman and a man were lying side by side, the girl on a cot and the man on the floor. The others sat within a few feet of them on the other side of the blankets, apparently lost to all sense of their danger, and too dejected and hope-less to even raise their eyes when I gave them money.

A fat little doctor was caring for the sick woman, and he pointed through the cracks in the floor at the green slime below us, and held his fingers to his nose and shrugged his shoulders. I asked him what ailed his patients, and he said it was yellow fever, and pointed again at the slime, which moved and bubbled in the hot sun.

He showed me babies with the skin drawn so tightly over their little bodies that the bones showed through as plainly as the rings under a glove. They were covered with sores, and they protested as loudly as they could against the treat-ment which the world was giving them, clinching their fists and sobbing with pain when the sore places came in contact with their mothers' arms. A planter who had at one time employed a large number of these people, and who was moving about among them, said that five hundred had died in Cardenas since the order to leave the fields had been issued. Another gentleman told me that in the huts at the back of the town there had been twenty-five cases of small-pox in one week, of which seventeen had resulted in death.

I do not know that the United States will interfere in the affairs of Cuba, but whatever may happen later, this is what is likely to happen now, and it should have some weight in helping to decide the question with those whose proper business it is to determine it.

Thousands of human beings are now herded together around the seaport towns of Cuba who cannot be fed, who have no knowledge of cleanliness or sanitation, who have no doctors to care for them and who cannot care for themselves.

Many of them are dying of sickness and some of starvation, and this is the healthy season. In April and May the rains will come, and the fever will thrive and spread, and cholera, yellow fever and small-pox will turn Cuba into one huge plague spot, and the farmers' sons whom Spain has sent over here to be soldiers, and who are dying by the dozens before they have learned to pull the comb off a bunch of cartridges, are going to die by the

hundreds, and women and children who are innocent of any offense will die with them, and there
will be a quarantine against Cuba, and no vessel
can come into her ports or leave them.

All this is going to happen, I am led to believe,
not from what I saw in any one village, but in hundreds of villages. It will not do to put it aside by
saying that "War is war," and that "All war is
cruel," or to ask, "Am I my brother's keeper?"

In other wars men have fought with men, and
women have suffered indirectly because the men
were killed, but in this war it is the women, herded
together in the towns like cattle, who are going to
die, while the men, camped in the fields and the
mountains, will live.

It is a situation which charity might help to better, but in any event it is a condition which deserves
the most serious consideration from men of common sense and judgment, and one not to be treated
with hysterical head lines nor put aside as a necessary evil of war.

The Death of Rodriguez

Bringing in the Wounded

The Death of Rodriguez

Adolfo Rodriguez was the only son of a Cuban farmer, who lives nine miles outside of Santa Clara, beyond the hills that surround that city to the north.

When the revolution broke out young Rodriguez joined the insurgents, leaving his father and mother and two sisters at the farm. He was taken, in December of 1896, by a force of the Guardia Civile, the corps d'élite of the Spanish army, and defended himself when they tried to capture him, wounding three of them with his machete.

He was tried by a military court for bearing arms against the government, and sentenced to be shot by a fusillade some morning, before sunrise.

Previous to execution, he was confined in the military prison of Santa Clara, with thirty other insurgents, all of whom were sentenced to be shot, one after the other, on mornings following the execution of Rodriguez.

His execution took place the morning of the 19th of January, at a place a half-mile distant from the city, on the great plain that stretches from the forts

out to the hills, beyond which Rodriguez had lived
for nineteen years.   At the time of his death he was
twenty years old.

I witnessed his execution, and what follows is an
account of the way he went to death.   The young
man's friends could not be present, for it was impossible for them to show themselves in that crowd
and that place with wisdom or without distress, and
I like to think that, although Rodriguez could not
know it, there was one person present when he died
who felt keenly for him, and who was a sympa-
thetic though unwilling spectator.

There had been a full moon the night preceding
the execution, and when the squad of soldiers
marched out from town it was still shining brightly
through the mists, although it was past five o'clock.
It lighted a plain two miles in extent broken by
ridges and gullies and covered with thick, high grass
and with bunches of cactus and palmetto.   In the
hollow of the ridges the mist lay like broad lakes of
water, and on one side of the plain stood the walls
of the old town.   On the other rose hills covered
with royal palms, that showed white in the moonlight, like hundreds of marble columns.   A line of
tiny camp fires that the sentries had built during the
night stretched between the forts at regular intervals and burned brightly.

But as the light grew stronger, and the moonlight faded, these were stamped out, and when the soldiers came in force the moon was a white ball in the sky, without radiance, the fires had sunk to ashes, and the sun had not yet risen.

So, even when the men were formed into three sides of a hollow square, they were scarcely able to distinguish one another in the uncertain light of the morning.

There were about three hundred soldiers in the formation. They belonged to the Volunteers, and they deployed upon the plain with their band in front, playing a jaunty quickstep, while their officers galloped from one side to the other through the grass, seeking out a suitable place for the execution, while the band outside the line still played merrily.

A few men and boys, who had been dragged out of their beds by the music, moved about the ridges, behind the soldiers, half-clothed, unshaven, sleepy-eyed, yawning and stretching themselves nervously and shivering in the cool, damp air of the morning.

Either owing to discipline or on account of the nature of their errand or because the men were still but half awake, there was no talking in the ranks, and the soldiers stood motionless, leaning on their rifles, with their backs turned to the town, looking out across the plain to the hills.

The men in the crowd behind them were also grimly silent. They knew that whatever they might say would be twisted into a word of sympathy for the condemned man or a protest against the government. So no one spoke; even the officers gave their orders in gruff whispers, and the men in the crowd did not mix together, but looked suspiciously at one another and kept apart.

As the light increased a mass of people came hurrying from the town with two black figures leading them, and the soldiers drew up at attention, and part of the double line fell back and left an opening in the square.

With us a condemned man walks only the short distance from his cell to the scaffold or the electric chair, shielded from sight by the prison walls; and it often occurs even then that the short journey is too much for his strength and courage.

But the merciful Spaniards on this morning made the prisoner walk for over a half-mile across the broken surface of the fields. I expected to find the man, no matter what his strength at other times might be, stumbling and faltering on this cruel journey, but as he came nearer I saw that he led

Young Spanish Officer

63

all the others, that the priests on either side of him were taking two steps to his one, and that they were tripping on their gowns and stumbling over the hollows, in their efforts to keep pace with him as he walked, erect and soldierly, at a quick step in advance of them.

He had a handsome, gentle face of the peasant type, a light, pointed beard, great wistful eyes and a mass of curly black hair. He was shockingly young for such a sacrifice, and looked more like a Neapolitan than a Cuban. You could imagine him sitting on the quay at Naples or Genoa, lolling in the sun and showing his white teeth when he laughed. He wore a new scapula around his neck, hanging outside his linen blouse.

It seems a petty thing to have been pleased with at such a time, but I confess to have felt a thrill of satisfaction when I saw, as the Cuban passed me, that he held a cigarette between his lips, not arrogantly nor with bravado, but with the nonchalance of a man who meets his punishment fearlessly, and who will let his enemies see that they can kill but can not frighten him.

It was very quickly finished, with rough, and, but for one frightful blunder, with merciful swiftness. The crowd fell back when it came to the square, and the condemned man, the priests and the firing squad of six young volunteers passed in and the line closed behind them.

The officer who had held the cord that bound the Cuban's arms behind him and passed across his breast, let it fall on the grass and drew his sword, and Rodriguez dropped his cigarette from his lips and bent and kissed the cross which the priest held up before him.

The elder of the priests moved to one side and prayed rapidly in a loud whisper, while the other, a younger man, walked away behind the firing squad and covered his face with his hands and turned his back. They had both spent the last twelve hours with Rodriguez in the chapel of the prison.

The Cuban walked to where the officer directed him to stand, and turned his back to the square and faced the hills and the road across them which led to his father's farm.

As the officer gave the first command he straightened himself as far as the cords would allow, and held up his head and fixed his eyes immovably on the morning light which had just begun to show above the hills.

He made a picture of such pathetic helplessness, but of such courage and dignity, that he reminded me on the instant of that statue of Nathan Hale, which stands in the City Hall Park, above the roar of

Broadway, and teaches a lesson daily to the hurrying crowds of moneymakers who pass beneath.

The Cuban's arms were bound, as are those of the statue, and he stood firmly, with his weight resting on his heels like a soldier on parade, and with his face held up fearlessly, as is that of the statue. But there was this difference, that Rodriguez, while probably as willing to give six lives for his country as was the American rebel, being only a peasant, did not think to say so, and he will not, in consequence, live in bronze during the lives of many men, but will be remembered only as one of thirty Cubans, one of whom was shot at Santa Clara on each succeeding day at sunrise.

The officer had given the order, the men had raised their pieces, and the condemned man had heard the clicks of the triggers as they were pulled back, and he had not moved. And then happened one of the most cruelly refined, though unintentional, acts of torture that one can very well imagine. As the officer slowly raised his sword, preparatory to giving the signal, one of the mounted officers rode up to him and pointed out silently what I had already observed with some satisfaction, that the firing squad were so placed that when they fired they would shoot several of the soldiers stationed on the extreme end of the square.

Their captain motioned his men to lower their pieces, and then walked across the grass and laid his hand on the shoulder of the waiting prisoner.

It is not pleasant to think what that shock must have been. The man had steeled himself to receive a volley of bullets in his back. He believed that in the next instant he would be in another world; he had heard the command given, had heard the click of the Mausers as the locks caught—and then, at that supreme moment, a human hand had been laid upon his shoulder and a voice spoke in his ear.

You would expect that any man who had been snatched back to life in such a fashion would start and tremble at the reprieve, or would break down altogether, but this boy turned his head steadily, and followed with his eyes the direction of the officer's sword, then nodded his head gravely, and, with his shoulders squared, took up a new position, straightened his back again, and once more held himself erect.

As an exhibition of self-control this should surely rank above feats of heroism performed in battle, where there are thousands of comrades to give inspiration. This man was alone, in the sight of the hills he knew, with only enemies about him, with no source to draw on for strength but that which lay within himself.

The Cuban Martyrdom

The officer of the firing squad, mortified by his blunder, hastily whipped up his sword, the men once more leveled their rifles, the sword rose, dropped, and the men fired. At the report the Cuban's head snapped back almost between his shoulders, but his body fell slowly, as though some one had pushed him gently forward from behind and he had stumbled.

He sank on his side in the wet grass without a struggle or sound, and did not move again.

It was difficult to believe that he meant to lie there, that it could be ended so without a word, that the man in the linen suit would not get up on his feet and continue to walk on over the hills, as he apparently had started to do, to his home; that there was not a mistake somewhere, or that at least some one would be sorry or say something or run to pick him up.

But, fortunately, he did not need help, and the priests returned—the younger one, with the tears running down his face—and donned their vestments and read a brief requiem for his soul, while the squad stood uncovered, and the men in hollow square shook their accoutrements into place, and shifted their pieces and got ready for the order to march, and the band began again with the same quickstep which the fusillade had interrupted.

The figure still lay on the grass untouched, and no one seemed to remember that it had walked there of itself, or noticed that the cigarette still burned, a tiny ring of living fire, at the place where the figure had first stood.

The figure was a thing of the past, and the squad shook itself like a great snake, and then broke into little pieces and started off jauntily, stumbling in the high grass and striving to keep step to the music.

The officers led it past the figure in the linen suit, and so close to it that the file closers had to part with the column to avoid treading on it. Each soldier as he passed turned and looked down on it, some craning their necks curiously, others giving a careless glance, and some without any interest at all, as they would have looked at a house by the roadside or a passing cart or a hole in the road.

One young soldier caught his foot in a trailing vine, and fell forward just opposite to it. He grew very red when his comrades giggled at him for his awkwardness. The crowd of sleepy spectators fell in on either side of the band. They had forgotten it, too, and the priests put their vestments back in the bag and wrapped their heavy cloaks about them, and hurried off after the others.

Every one seemed to have forgotten it except

two men, who came slowly toward it from the town, driving a bullock cart that bore an unplaned coffin, each with a cigarette between his lips, and with his throat wrapped in a shawl to keep out the morning mists.

At that moment the sun, which had shown some promise of its coming in the glow above the hills, shot up suddenly from behind them in all the splendor of the tropics, a fierce, red disc of heat, and filled the air with warmth and light.

The bayonets of the retreating column flashed in it, and at the sight of it a rooster in a farmyard near by crowed vigorously and a dozen bugles answered the challenge with the brisk, cheery notes of the reveille, and from all parts of the city the church bells jangled out the call for early mass, and the whole world of Santa Clara seemed to stir and stretch itself and to wake to welcome the day just begun.

But as I fell in at the rear of the procession and looked back the figure of the young Cuban, who was no longer a part of the world of Santa Clara, was asleep in the wet grass, with his motionless arms still tightly bound behind him, with the scapula twisted awry across his face and the blood from his breast sinking into the soil he had tried to free.

Along the Trocha

Regular Cavalryman—Spanish

Along the Trocha

This is an account of a voyage of discovery along the Spanish trocha, the one at the eastern end of Cuba. It is the longer of the two, and stretches from coast to coast at the narrowest part of that half of the island, from Jucaro on the south to Moron on the north.

Before I came to Cuba this time I had read in our newspapers about the Spanish trocha without knowing just what a trocha was. I imagined it to be a rampart of earth and fallen trees, topped with barbed wire; a Rubicon that no one was allowed to pass, but which the insurgents apparently crossed at will with the ease of little girls leaping over a flying skipping rope. In reality it seems to be a much more important piece of engineering than is generally supposed, and one which, when completed, may prove an absolute barrier to the progress of large bodies of troops unless they are supplied with artillery.

I saw twenty-five of its fifty miles, and the engineers in charge told me that I was the first American, or foreigner of any nationality, who had been

allowed to visit it and make drawings and photographs of it.   Why they allowed me to see it I do
not know, nor can I imagine either why they should
have objected to my doing so.   There is no great
mystery about it.

Indeed, what impressed me most concerning
it was the fact that every bit of material used in
constructing this backbone of the Spanish defence,
this strategic point of all their operations, and their
chief hope of success against the revolutionists, was
furnished by their despised and hated enemies in
the United States.   Every sheet of armor plate,
every corrugated zinc roof, every roll of barbed
wire, every plank, beam, rafter and girder, even the
nails that hold the planks together, the forts themselves, shipped in sections, which are numbered in
readiness for setting up, the ties for the military railroad which clings to the trocha from one sea to the
other—all of these have been supplied by manufac-
turers in the United States.

This is interesting when one remembers that the
American in the Spanish illustrated papers is represented as a hog, and generally with the United
States flag for trousers, and Spain as a noble and
valiant lion.   Yet it would appear that the lion is
willing to save a few dollars on freight by buying
his armament from his hoggish neighbor, and that

the American who cheers for Cuba Libre is not at all averse to making as many dollars as he can in building the wall against which the Cubans may be eventually driven and shot.

If the insurgents have found as much difficulty in crossing the trocha by land as I found in reaching it by water, they are deserving of all sympathy as patient and long-suffering individuals.

A thick jungle stretches for miles on either side of the trocha, and the only way of reaching it from the outer world is through the seaports at either end. Of these, Moron is all but landlocked, and Jucaro is guarded by a chain of keys, which make it necessary to reship all the troops and their supplies and all the material for the trocha to lighters, which meet the vessels six miles out at sea.

A dirty Spanish steamer drifted with us for two nights and a day from Cienfuegos to Jucaro, and three hundred Spanish soldiers, dusty, ragged and barefooted, owned her as completely as though she had been a regular transport. They sprawled at full length over every deck, their guns were stacked in each corner, and their hammocks swung four deep from railings and riggings and across companionways, and even from the bridge itself. It was not possible to take a step without treading on one of them, and their hammocks made a walk on the deck something like a hurdle race.

With the soldiers, and crowding them for space, were the officers' mules and ponies, steers, calves and squealing pigs, while crates full of chickens were piled on top of one another as high as the hurricane deck, so that the roosters and the buglers vied with each other in continual contests. It was like traveling with a floating menagerie. Twice a day the bugles sounded the call for breakfast and dinner, and the soldiers ceased to sprawl, and squatted on the deck around square tin cans filled with soup or red wine, from which they fed themselves with spoons and into which they dipped their rations of hard tack, after first breaking them on the deck with a blow from a bayonet or crushing them with a rifle butt.

The steward brought what was supposed to be a sample of this soup to the officer seated in the pilot house high above the squalor, and he would pick out a bean from the mess on the end of a fork and place it to his lips and nod his head gravely, and the grinning steward would carry the dish away.

But the soldiers seemed to enjoy it very much, and to be content, even cheerful. There are many things to admire about the Spanish Tommy. In the seven fortified cities which I visited, where there

One of the Block Houses

From a photograph taken by Mr. Davis

were thousands of him, I never saw one drunk or aggressive, which is much more than you can say of his officers. On the march he is patient, eager and alert. He trudges from fifteen to thirty miles a day over the worst roads ever constructed by man, in canvas shoes with rope soles, carrying one hundred and fifty cartridges, fifty across his stomach and one hundred on his back, weighing in all fifty pounds.

With these he has his Mauser, his blanket and an extra pair of shoes, and as many tin plates and bottles and bananas and potatoes and loaves of white bread as he can stow away in his blouse and knapsack. And this under a sun which makes even a walking stick seem a burden. In spite of his officers, and not on account of them, he maintains good discipline, and no matter how tired he may be or how much he may wish to rest on his plank bed, he will always struggle to his feet when the officers pass, and stand at salute. He gets very little in return for his efforts.

One Sunday night, when the band was playing in the plaza, at a heaven-forsaken fever camp called Ciego de Avila, a group of soldiers were sitting near me on the grass enjoying the music. They loitered there a few minutes after the bugle had sounded the retreat to the barracks, and the officer

of the day found them.   When they stood up he
ordered them to report themselves at the *cartel*
under arrest, and then, losing all control of himself,
lashed one little fellow over the head with his colonel's staff, while the boy stood with his eyes shut
and with his lips pressed together, but holding his
hand at salute until the officer's stick beat it down.

These soldiers are from the villages and towns
of Spain; some of them are not more than seventeen years old, and they are not volunteers.   They
do not care whether Spain owns an island eighty
miles from the United States, or loses it, but they
go out to it and have their pay stolen, and are put
to building earth forts and stone walls, and die of
fever.   It seems a poor return for their unconscious
patriotism when a colonel thrashes one of them as
though he were a dog, especially as he knows the
soldier may not strike back.

The second night out the ship steward showed
us a light lying low in the water, and told us that
was Jucaro, and we accepted his statement and
went over the side into an open boat, in which we
drifted about until morning, while the colored man
who owned the boat, and a little mulatto boy who
steered it, quarreled as to where exactly the town
of Jucaro might be.   They brought us up at last
against a dark shadow of a house, built on wooden

Spanish Cavalry

From photographs taken by Mr. Davis

posts, and apparently floating in the water. This was the town of Jucaro as seen at that hour of the night, and as we left it before sunrise the next morning, I did not know until my return whether I had slept in a stationary ark or on the end of a wharf.

We found four other men sleeping on the floor in the room assigned us, and outside, eating by a smoking candle, a young English boy, who looked up and laughed when he heard us speak, and said:

"You've come at last, have you? You are the first white men I've seen since I came here. That's twelve months ago."

He was the cable operator at Jucaro; and he sits all day in front of a sheet of white paper, and watches a ray of light play across an imaginary line, and he can tell by its quivering, so he says, all that is going on all over the world. Outside of his whitewashed cable office is the landlocked bay, filled with wooden piles to keep out the sharks, and back of him lies the village of Jucaro, consisting of two open places filled with green slime and filth and thirty huts. But the operator said that what with fishing and bathing and "Tit-Bits" and "Lloyd's Weekly Times," Jucaro was quite enjoyable. He is going home the year after this.

"At least, that's how I put it," he explained. "My contract requires me to stop on here until December of 1898, but it doesn't sound so long if you say 'a year after this,' does it?" He had had the yellow fever, and had never, owing to the war, been outside of Jucaro. "Still," he added, "I'm seeing the world, and I've always wanted to visit foreign parts."

As one of the few clean persons I met in Cuba, and the only contented one, I hope the cable operator at Jucaro will get a rise in salary soon, and some day see more of foreign parts than he is seeing at present, and at last get back to "the Horse Shoe, at the corner of Tottenham Court Road and Oxford street, sir," where, as we agreed, better entertainment is to be had on Saturday night than anywhere in London.

In Havana, General Weyler had given me a pass to enter fortified places, which, except for the authority which the signature implied, meant nothing, as all the cities and towns in Cuba are fortified, and any one can visit them. It was as though Mayor Strong had given a man a permit to ride in all the cable cars attached to cables.

It was not intended to include the trocha, but I argued that if a trocha was not a "fortified place" nothing else was, and I persuaded the comman-

One of the Forts Along the Trocha

From photograph taken by Mr. Davis

dante at Jucaro to take that view of it and to visé
Weyler's order. So at five the following morning a
box car, with wooden planks stretched across it for
seats, carried me along the line of the trocha from
Jucaro to Ciego, the chief military port on the for-
tifications, and consumed five hot and stifling hours
in covering twenty-five miles.

The trocha is a cleared space, one hundred and
fifty to two hundred yards wide, which stretches for
fifty miles through what is apparently an impassable jungle. The trees which have been cut down
in clearing this passageway have been piled up at
either side of the cleared space and laid in parallel
rows, forming a barrier of tree trunks and roots
and branches as wide as Broadway and higher than
a man's head. It would take a man some time to
pick his way over these barriers, and a horse could
no more do it than it could cross a jam of floating
logs in a river.

Between the fallen trees lies the single track of
the military railroad, and on one side of that is the
line of forts and a few feet beyond them a maze of
barbed wire. Beyond the barbed wire again is
the other barrier of fallen trees and the jungle. In
its unfinished state this is not an insurmountable
barricade. Gomez crossed it last November by
daylight with six hundred men, and with but the

loss of twenty-seven killed and as many wounded.
To-day it would be more difficult, and in a few
months, without the aid of artillery, it will be
impossible, except with the sacrifice of a great loss
of life. The forts are of three kinds. They are best
described as the forts, the block houses and the little forts. A big fort consists of two stories, with a
cellar below and a watch tower above. It is made
of stone and adobe, and is painted a glaring
white. One of these is placed at intervals of every
half mile along the trocha, and on a clear day the
sentry in the watch tower of each can see three forts
on either side.

Midway between the big forts, at a distance of a
quarter of a mile from each, is a block house of two
stories with the upper story of wood, overhanging
the lower foundation of mud. These are placed at
right angles to the railroad, instead of facing it, as
do the forts.

Between each block house and each fort are three
little forts of mud and planks, surrounded by a
ditch. They look something like a farmer's ice
house as we see it at home, and they are about as
hot inside as the other is cold. They hold five men,
and are within hailing distance of one another.
Back of them are three rows of stout wooden
stakes, with barbed wire stretching from one row

to the other, interlacing and crossing and running in and out above and below, like an intricate cat's cradle of wire.

One can judge how closely knit it is by the fact that to every twelve yards of posts there are four hundred and fifty yards of wire fencing. The forts are most completely equipped in their way, but twelve men in the jungle would find it quite easy to keep twelve men securely imprisoned in one of them for an indefinite length of time.

The walls are about twelve feet high, with a cellar below and a vault above the cellar. The roof of the vault forms a platform, around which the four walls rise to the height of a man's shoulder. There are loopholes for rifles in the sides of the vault, and where the platform joins the walls. These latter allow the men in the fort to fire down almost directly upon the head of any one' who comes up close to the wall of the fort, where, without these holes in the floor, it would be impossible to fire on him except by leaning far over the rampart.

Above the platform is an iron or zinc roof, supported by iron pillars, and in the centre of this is the watch tower. The only approach to the fort is by a movable ladder, which hangs over the side like the gangway of a ship of war, and can be

raised by those on the inside by means of a rope
suspended over a wheel in the roof. The opening
in the wall at the head of the ladder is closed at
the time of an attack by an iron platform, to which
the ladder leads, and which also can be raised by a
pulley. In October of 1897 the Spanish hope to
have calcium lights placed in the watch towers of
the forts with sufficient power to throw a search-
light over a quarter of a mile, or to the next block
house, and so keep the trocha as well lighted as
Broadway from one end to the other.

As a further protection against the insurgents
the Spaniards have distributed a number of bombs
along the trocha, which they showed with great
pride. These are placed at those points along the
trocha where the jungle is less thickly grown, and
where the insurgents might be expected to pass.

Each bomb is fitted with an explosive cap, to
which five or six wires are attached and staked
down on the ground. Any one stumbling over
one of these wires explodes the bomb and throws
a charge of broken iron to a distance of fifty feet.
How the Spaniards are going to prevent stray
cattle and their own soldiers from wandering into
these man-traps it is difficult to understand.

The chief engineer in charge of the trocha detailed a captain to take me over it and to show me

The Trocha

From a photograph taken by Mr. Davis

all that there was to see. The officers of the infantry and cavalry stationed at Ciego objected to his doing this, but he said: "He has a pass from General Weyler. I am not responsible." It was true that I had an order from General Weyler, but he had rendered it ineffective by having me followed about wherever I went by his police and spies. They sat next to me in the cafés and in the plazas, and when I took a cab they called the next one on the line and trailed after mine all around the city, until my driver would become alarmed for fear he, too, was suspected of something, and would take me back to the hotel.

I had gotten rid of them at Cienfuegos by purchasing a ticket on the steamer to Santiago, three days further down the coast, and then dropping off in the night at the trocha, so while I was visiting it I expected to find that my non-arrival at Santiago had been reported, and word sent to the trocha that I was a newspaper correspondent. And whenever an officer spoke to the one who was showing me about, my camera appeared to grow to the size of a trunk, and to weigh like lead, and I felt lonely, and longed for the company of the cheerful cable operator at the other end of the trocha.

But as I had seen Mr. Gillette in "Secret Service" only seventeen times before leaving New

York, I knew just what to do, which was to smoke all the time and keep cool. The latter requirement was somewhat difficult, as Ciego de Avila is a hotter place than Richmond. Indeed, I can only imagine one place hotter than Ciego, and I have not been there.

Ciego was an interesting town. During every day of the last rainy season an average of thirty soldiers and officers died there of yellow fever. While I was there I saw two soldiers, one quite an old man, drop down in the street as though they had been shot, and lie in the road until they were carried to the yellow fever ward of the hospital, under the black oilskin cloth of the stretchers.

There was a very smart officers' club at Ciego well supplied with a bar and billiard tables, which I made some excuse for not entering, but which could be seen through its open doors, and I suggested to one of the members that it must be a comfort to have such a place, where the officers might go after their day's march on the mud banks of the trocha, and where they could bathe and be cool and clean. He said there were no baths in the club nor anywhere in the town. He added that he thought it might be a good idea to have them.

The bath tub is the dividing line between savages and civilized beings. And when I learned that regiment after regiment of Spanish officers and gentlemen have been stationed in that town—and it was the dirtiest, hottest and dustiest town I ever visited—for eighteen months, and none of them had wanted a bath, I believed from that moment all the stories I had heard about their butcheries and atrocities, stories which I had verified later by more direct evidence.

From a military point of view the trocha impressed me as a weapon which could be made to cut both ways. What the Spaniards think of it is shown by the caricature which appeared lately in "Don Quixote," and which shows the United States represented by a hog and the insurgents represented by a negro imprisoned in the trocha, while Weyler stands ready to turn the Spanish lion on them and watch it gobble them up.

It would be unkind were Spain to do anything so inconsiderate, and besides, the United States is rather a large mouthful even without the insurgents who taken alone seem to have given the lion some pangs of indigestion.

If the trocha were situated on a broad plain or prairie with a mile of clear ground on either side of it, where troops could manœuvre, and which would prevent the enemy from stealing up to it unseen, it might be a useful line of defence. But at present, along its entire length, stretches this almost impassable barrier of jungle. Now suppose the troops are sent at short notice from the military camps along the line to protect any particular point?

Not less than a thousand soldiers must be sent forward, and one can imagine what their condition would be were they forced to manœuvre in a space one hundred and fifty yards broad, the half of which is taken up with barbed wire fences, fallen trees and explosive bomb shells. Only two hundred at the most could find shelter in the forts, which would mean that eight hundred men would be left outside the breastworks and scattered over a distance of a half mile, with a forest on both sides of them, from which the enemy could fire volley after volley into their ranks, protected from pursuit not only by the jungle, but by the walls of fallen trees which the Spaniards themselves have placed there.

A trocha in an open plain, as were the English trochas in the desert around Suakin, makes an admirable defence, when a few men are forced to withstand the assault of a great many, but fighting behind a trocha in a jungle is like fighting in an ambush, and if the trocha at Moron is ever attacked in force it will prove to be a Valley of Death to the Spanish troops.

The Question of
Atrocities

Spanish Troops in Action

102

The Question of Atrocities

One of the questions that is most frequently asked of those who have been in Cuba is how much truth exists in the reports of Spanish butcheries. It is safe to say in answer to this that while the report of a particular atrocity may not be true, other atrocities just as horrible have occurred and nothing has been heard of them. I was somewhat skeptical of Spanish atrocities until I came to Cuba, chiefly because I had been kept sufficiently long in Key West to learn how large a proportion of Cuban war news is manufactured on the piazzas of the hotels of that town and of Tampa by utterly irresponsible newspaper men who accept every rumor that finds its way across the gulf, and pass these rumors on to some of the New York papers as facts coming direct from the field.

It is not surprising that one becomes skeptical, for if one story proves to be false, how is the reader to know that the others are not inventions also?

It is difficult to believe, for instance, the account of a horrible butchery if you read in the paragraph above it that two correspondents have been taken prisoners by the Spanish, when both of these gentlemen are sitting beside you in Key West and are, to your certain knowledge, reading the paragraph over your shoulder. Nor is it unnatural that one should grow doubtful of reported Cuban victories if he reads of the taking of Santa Clara and the flight of the Spanish garrison from that city, when he is living at Santa Clara and cannot find a Cuban in it with sufficient temerity to assist him to get out of it through the Spanish lines.

But because a Jacksonville correspondent has invented the tale of one butchery, it is no reason why the people in the United States should dismiss all the others as sensational fictions. After I went to Cuba I refused for weeks to listen to tales of butcheries, because I did not believe in them and because there seemed to be no way of verifying them—those who had been butchered could not testify and their relatives were too fearful of the vengeance of the Spaniards to talk about what had befallen a brother or a father. But towards the end of my visit I went to Sagua la Grande and there met a number of Americans and Englishmen, concerning whose veracity there

could be no question.   What had happened to
their friends and the laborers on their plantations
was exactly what had happened and is happening
to-day to other pacificos all over the island.

Sagua la Grande is probably no worse a city
than others in Cuba, but it has been rendered
notorious by the presence in that city of the guerrilla chieftain, Benito Cerreros.

Early in last December *Leslie's Illustrated Weekly*
published half-tone reproductions of two photographs which were taken in Sagua. One was a picture of the bodies of six Cuban pacificos lying on
their backs, with their arms and legs bound and
their bodies showing mutilation by machetes, and
their faces pounded and hacked out of resemblance
to anything human. The other picture was of a
group of Spanish guerrillas surrounding their
leader, a little man with a heavy mustache.   His
face was quite as inhuman as the face of any of the
dead men he had mutilated. It wore a satisfied smile
of fatuous vanity, and of the most diabolical cruelty.
No artist could have drawn a face from his imagina-
tion which would have been more cruel. The
letter press accompanying these photographs
explained that this guerrilla leader, Benito Cerreros, had found six unarmed pacificos working in a
field near Sagua, and had murdered them and then

brought their bodies in a cart to that town, and had paid the local photographer to take a picture of them and of himself and his body guard. He claimed that he had killed the Cubans in open battle, but was so stupid as to forget to first remove the ropes with which he had bound them before he shot them. The photographs told the story without any aid from the letter press, and it must have told it to a great many people, judging from the number who spoke of it. It seemed as if, for the first time, something definite regarding the reported Spanish atrocities had been placed before the people of the United States, which they could see for themselves. I had this photograph in my mind when I came to Sagua, and on the night that I arrived there, by a coincidence, the townspeople were giving Cerreros a dinner to celebrate a fresh victory of his over two insurgents, a naturalized American and a native Cuban.

The American was visiting the Cuban in the field, and they were lying in hiding outside of the town in a hut. The Cuban, who was a colonel in the insurgent army, had captured a Spanish spy, but had given him his liberty on the condition that he would go into Sagua and bring back some medicines. The colonel was dying of consumption, but he hoped that, with proper medicine, he might re-

Amateur Surgery in Cuba

main alive a few months longer. The spy, instead of keeping his word, betrayed the hiding place of the Cuban and the American to Cerreros, who rode out by night to surprise them. He took with him thirty-two guerrillas, and, lest that might not be enough to protect him from two men, added twelve of the Guarda Civile to their number, making forty-four men in all. They surrounded the hut in which the Cuban and the American were concealed, and shot them through the window as they sat at a table in the light of a candle. They then hacked the bodies with machetes. It was in recognition of this victory that the banquet was tendered to Cerreros by admiring friends.

Civilized nations recognize but three methods of dealing with prisoners captured in war. They are either paroled or exchanged or put in prison; that is what was done with them in our rebellion. It is not allowable to shoot prisoners; at least it is not generally done when they are seated unconscious of danger at a table. It may be said, however, that, as these two men were in arms against the government, they were only suffering the punishment of their crime, and that this is not a good instance of an atrocity. There are, however, unfortunately, many other instances in which the victims were non-combatants and their death simply murder. But it is extremely difficult to tell convincingly of these cases, without giving names, and the giving of names might lead to more deaths in Sagua. It is also difficult to convince the reader of murders for which there seems to have been no possible object.

And yet Cerreros and other guerrillas are murdering men and boys in the fields around Sagua as wantonly and as calmly as a gardener cuts down weeds. The stories of these butcheries were told to me by Englishmen and Americans who could look from their verandas over miles of fields that belonged to them, but who could not venture with safety two hundred yards from their doorsteps. They were virtually prisoners in their own homes, and every spot of ground within sight of their windows marked where one of their laborers had been cut down, sometimes when he was going to the next *central* on an errand, or to carry the mail, and sometimes when he was digging potatoes or cutting sugar cane within sight of the forts. Passes and orders were of no avail. The guerrillas tore up the passes, and swore later that the men were suspects, and were at the moment of their capture carrying messages to the insurgents. The stories these planters told me were not dragged from them to furnish copy for a newspaper, but came out in the course of our talk, as we walked over the small extent which the forts allowed us.

My host would say, pointing to one of the pacificos huddled in a corner of his machine shop: "That man's brother was killed last week about three hundred yards over there to the left while he was digging in the field." Or, in answer to a question from our consul, he would say: "Oh, that boy who used to take care of your horse—some guerrillas shot him a month ago." After you hear stories like these during an entire day, the air seems to be heavy with murder, and the very ground on which you walk smells of blood. It was the same in the town, where any one was free to visit the *cartel*, and view the murdered bodies of the pacificos hacked and beaten and stretched out as a warning, or for public approbation. There were six so exposed while I was in Sagua. In Matanzas they brought the bodies to the Plaza at night when the band was playing, and the guerrillas marched around the open place with the bodies of eighteen Cubans swinging from the backs of ponies with their heads hanging down and bumping against the horses' knees. The people flocked to the sides of the Plaza to applaud this ghastly procession, and the men in the open cafés cheered the guerrilla chief and cried, "Long live Spain!"

Speaking dispassionately, and with a full knowledge of the details of many butcheries, it is impossible for me to think of the Spanish guerrillas otherwise than as worse than savage animals. A wild animal kills to obtain food, and not merely for the joy of killing. These guerrillas murder and then laugh over it. The cannibal, who has been supposed hitherto to be the lowest grade of man, is really of a higher caste than these Spanish murderers—men like Colonel Fondevila, Cerreros, and Colonel Bonita—for a cannibal kills to keep himself alive. These men kill to feed their vanity, in order that they may pose as brave soldiers, and that their friends may give them banquets in hotel parlors.

If what I say seems prejudiced and extravagant it may be well to insert this translation from a Spanish paper, *El Pais*:

"There are signs of civilization among us; but the truth is that we are uncultured, barbaric and cruel. Although this may not be willingly acknowledged, the fact is that we are committing acts of savagery of which there is no counterpart in any other European country.

"Let us not say a word of the atrocities perpetrated at the Castle of Montjuich; of the iniquitous and miserable massacre of the Novelda republicans; of the shootings which occur daily in Manila; of the

Scouting Party of Spanish Cavalry

113

arbitrary imprisonments which are systematically made here. We wish now to say something of the respect due to the conquered, of generosity that should be shown to prisoners of war, for these are sentiments which exist even among savage people.

"The Cuban exiles who disembark at Cadiz are sent on foot to the distant castle of Figueras. 'The unfortunate exiles,' a letter from Carpio says, 'passed here barefooted and bleeding, almost naked and freezing. At every town, far from finding rest for their fatigue, they are received with all sorts of insults; they are scoffed and provoked. I am indignant at this total lack of humanitarian sentiment and charity. I have two sons who are fighting against the Cuban insurgents; but this does not prevent me from denouncing those who ill-treat their prisoners. I have witnessed such outrages upon the unfortunate exiles that I do not hesitate to say that nothing like it has ever occurred in Africa.'"

I do not wish what I have said concerning the Florida correspondents to be misunderstood as referring to those who are writing, and have written from the island of Cuba. They suffer from the "fakirs" even more than do the people of the United States who read the stories of both, and who confound the sensation-mongers with those who go to find the truth at the risk of their lives. For these latter do risk their lives, daily and hourly, when they go into these conflicts looking for the facts. I have not been in any conflict, so I can speak of these men without fear of being misunderstood.

They are taking chances that no war correspondents ever took in any war in any part of the world. For this is not a war—it is a state of lawless butchery, and the rights of correspondents, of soldiers and of non-combatants are not recognized. Archibald Forbes, and "Bull Run" Russell and Frederick Villiers had great continental armies to protect them; these men work alone with a continental army against them. They risk capture at sea and death by the guns of a Spanish cruiser, and, escaping that, they face when they reach the island the greater danger of capture there and of being cut down by a guerrilla force and left to die in a road, or of being put in a prison and left to die of fever, as Govin was cut down, as Delgardo died in prison, as Melton is lying in prison now, where he will continue to lie until we have a Secretary of State who recognizes the rights of the correspondent as a non-combatant, or at least as an American citizen.

The fate of these three American correspondents has not deterred others from crossing the lines, and they are in the field now, lying in swamps by day and creeping between the forts by night, standing under fire by the side of Gomez as they stood beside Maceo, going without food, without shelter, without the right to answer the attacks of the Spanish troops, climbing the mountains and crawling across the trochas, creeping to some friendly hut for a cup of coffee and to place their despatches in safe hands, and then going back again to run the gauntlet of Spanish spies and of flying columns and of the unspeakable guerrillas.

When you sit comfortably at your breakfast in New York, with a policeman at the corner, and read the despatches which these gentlemen write of Cuban victories and their interviews with self-important Cuban chiefs, you should remember what it cost them to supply you with that addition to your morning's budget of news. Whether the result is worth the risk, or whether it is not paying too great a price, the greatest price of all, for too little, is not the question. The reckless bravery and the unselfishness of the correspondents in the field in Cuba to-day are beyond parallel.

It is as dangerous to seek for Gomez as Stanley found it to seek for Livingston, and as few men return from the insurgent camps as from the Arctic regions.

In case you do not read a New York paper, it is

well that you should know that the names of these
correspondents are Grover Flint, Sylvester Scovel
and George Bronson Rae. I repeat, that as I could
not reach the field, I can write thus freely of those
who have been more successful.

The Right of Search of American Vessels

An Officer of Spanish Guerillas

The Right of Search of American Vessels

On the boat which carried me from Cuba to Key West were three young girls, who had been exiled for giving aid to the insurgents. The brother of one of them is in command of the Cuban forces in the field near Havana. More than once his sister had joined him there, and had seen fighting and carried back despatches to the Junta in Havana. For this she and two other young women, who were also suspected, were ordered to leave the island.

I happened to sit next to this young lady at table on the steamer, and I found that she was not an Amazon nor a Joan of Arc nor a woman of the people, with a machete in one hand and a Cuban flag in the other. She was a well-bred, well-educated young person, speaking three languages.

This is what the Spaniards did to these girls:

After ordering them to leave the island on a certain day they sent detectives to the houses of each on the morning of that day and had them undressed and searched by a female detective to discover if they were carrying letters to the Junta at Key West or Tampa. They were seached thoroughly, even to the length of taking off their shoes and stockings. Later, when the young ladies stood at last on the deck of an American vessel, with the American flag hanging from the stern, the Spanish officers followed them there, and demanded that a cabin should be furnished them to which the girls might be taken, and they were then again undressed and searched by this woman for the second time.

For the benefit of people with unruly imaginations, of whom there seem to be a larger proportion in this country than I had supposed, I will state again that the search of these women was conducted by women and not by men, as I was reported to have said, and as I did not say in my original report of the incident.

Spanish officers, with red crosses for bravery on their chests and gold lace on their cuffs, strutted up and down while the search was going on, and chancing to find a Cuban suspect among the passengers, ordered him to be searched also, only they did not give him the privacy of a cabin, but searched his clothes and shoes and hat on the main deck of this American vessel before the other passengers and myself and the ship's captain and his crew.

In order to leave Havana, it is first necessary to give notice of your wish to do so by sending your passport to the Captain General, who looks up your record, and, after twenty-four hours, if he is willing to let you go, visés your passport and so signifies that your request is granted. After you have complied with that requirement of martial law, and the Captain General has agreed to let you depart, and you are on board of an American vessel, the Spanish soldiers' control over you and your movements should cease, for they relinquish all their rights when they give you back your passport.

At least the case of Barrundia justifies such a supposition. It was then shown that, while a passenger or a member of a crew is amenable to the "common laws" of the country in the port in which the vessel lies, he is not to be disturbed for political offenses against her government.

When the officers of Guatemala went on board a vessel of the Pacific Mail line and arrested Barrundia, who was a revolutionist, and then shot him between decks, the American Minister, who had permitted this outrage, was immediately recalled, and the letter recalling him, which was written by James G. Blaine, clearly and emphatically sets forth the principle that a political offender is not to be molested on board of an American vessel, whether she is in the passenger trade or a ship of war.

Prof. Joseph H. Beale, Jr., the professor of international law at Harvard, said in reference to the case of these women when I first wrote of it:

"So long as a state of war has not been recognized by this country, the Spanish government has not the right to stop or search our vessels on the high seas for contraband of war or for any other purpose, nor would it have the right to subject American citizens or an American vessel in Cuban waters to treatment which would not be legal in the case of Spanish citizens or vessels.

"But the Spanish government has the right in Cuba to execute upon American citizens or vessels any laws prevailing there, in the same way as they would execute them upon the Spaniards, unless they are prevented by the provisions of some treaty with the United States. The fact that the vessel in the harbor of Havana was flying a neutral flag could not protect it from the execution of Spanish law.

"However unwise or inhuman the action of the Spanish authorities may have been in searching the women on board the *Olivette*, they appear to have been within their legal rights."

A Spanish Picket Post

The Spanish Minister at Washington has also declared that his government has the right of search in the harbor of Havana. Hence in the face of two such authorities the question raised is probably answered from a legal point of view. But if that is the law, it would seem well to alter it, for it gives the Spanish authorities absolute control over the persons and property of Americans on American vessels, and that privilege in the hands of persons as unscrupulous and as insolent as are the Spanish detectives, is a dangerous one. So dangerous a privilege, indeed, that there is no reason nor excuse for not keeping an American ship of war in the harbor of Havana.

For suppose that letters and despatches had been found on the persons of these young ladies, and they had been put on shore and lodged in prison; or suppose the whole ship and every one on board had been searched, as the captain of the *Olivette* said the Spanish officers told him they might decide to do, and letters had been found on the Americans, and they had been ordered over the side and put into prison—would that have been an act derogatory to the dignity of the United States? Or are we to understand that an American citizen or a citizen of any country, after he has asked and obtained permission to leave Cuba and is on board

of an American vessel, is no more safe there than
he would be in the insurgent camp?

The latter supposition would seem to be correct,
and the matter to depend on the captain of the vessel and her owners, from whom he receives his in-
structions, and not to be one in which the United
States government is in any way concerned.   I do
not believe the captain of a British passenger
steamer would have allowed one of his passengers
to be searched on the main deck of his vessel, as I
saw this Cuban searched; nor even the captain of
a British tramp steamer nor of a coal barge.

The chief engineer of the *Olivette* declared to me
that in his opinion, "it served them just right," and
the captain put a cabin at the disposal of the Spanish spies with eager humility.   And when one of
the detectives showed some disinclination to give
back my passport, and I said I would keep him on
board until he did it, the captain said: "Yes, you
will, will you?   I would like to see you try it," sug-
gesting that he was master of his own ship and of
my actions.   But he was not.   There is not an
unwashed, garlicky, bediamonded Spanish spy in
Cuba who has not more authority on board the
Olivette than her American captain and his subser-
vient crew.

Only a year ago half of this country was clamor-

ing for a war with the greatest power it could have
selected for that purpose. Yet Great Britain
would have been the first to protect her citizens and their property and their self-respect if
they had been abused as the self-respect and property and freedom of Americans have been abused
by this fourth-rate power, and are being abused
to-day.

Before I went to Cuba I was as much opposed to
our interfering there as any other person equally
ignorant concerning the situation could be, but
since I have seen for myself I feel ashamed that we
should have stood so long idle. We have been too
considerate, too fearful that as a younger nation, we
should appear to disregard the laws laid down by
older nations. We have tolerated what no European power would have tolerated; we have been
patient with men who have put back the hand of
time for centuries, who lie to our representatives
daily, who butcher innocent people, who gamble
with the lives of their own soldiers in order to gain
a few more stars and an extra stripe, who send
American property to the air in flames and murder
American prisoners.

The British lately sent an expedition of eight
hundred men to the west coast of Africa to punish
a savage king who butchers people because it does

not rain. Why should we tolerate Spanish savages merely because they call themselves "the most Catholic," but who in reality are no better than this naked negro? What difference is there between the King of Benin who crucifies a woman because he wants rain and General Weyler who outrages a woman for his own pleasure and throws her to his bodyguard of blacks, even if the woman has the misfortune to live after it—and to still live in Sagua la Grande to-day?

If the English were right—and they were right—in punishing the King of Benin for murdering his subjects to propitiate his idols, we are right to punish these revivers of the Inquisition for starving women and children to propitiate an Austrian archduchess.

It is difficult to know what the American people do want. They do not want peace, apparently, for their senators, some through an ignorant hatred of England and others through a personal dislike of the President, emasculated the arbitration treaty; and they do not want war, for, as some one has written, if we did not go to war with Spain when she murdered the crew of the *Virginius*, we never will.

But if the executive and the legislators wish to assure themselves, like "Fighting Bob Acres," that

Frederic Remington.

General Weyler in the Field

they have some right on their side, they need not turn back to the *Virginius* incident. There are reasons enough to-day to justify their action, if it is to be their intellects and not their feelings that must move them to act. American property has been destroyed by Spanish troops to the amount of many millions, and no answer made to demands of the State Department for an explanation. American citizens have been imprisoned and shot—some without a trial, some in front of their own domiciles, and American vessels are turned over to the uses of the Spanish secret police. These would seem to be sufficient reasons for interfering.

But why should we not go a step farther and a step higher, and interfere in the name of humanity? Not because we are Americans, but because we are human beings, and because, within eighty miles of our coast, Spanish officials are killing men and women as wantonly as though they were field mice, not in battle, but in cold blood—cutting them down in the open roads, at the wells to which they have gone for water, or on their farms, where they have stolen away to dig up a few potatoes, having first run the gauntlets of the forts and risked their lives to obtain them.

This is not an imaginary state of affairs, nor are these supposititious cases. I am writing only of the things I have heard from eye witnesses and of some of the things that I have seen.

President Cleveland declared in his message to Congress: "When the inability of Spain to deal successfully with the insurgents has become manifest, and it is demonstrated that her sovereignty is extinct in Cuba for all purposes of its rightful existence, and when a hopeless struggle for its re-establishment has degenerated into a strife which is nothing more than the useless sacrifice of human life and the utter destruction of the very subject-matter of the conflict, a situation will be presented in which our obligations to the sovereignty of Spain will be superseded by higher obligations, which we can hardly hesitate to recognize and discharge!"

These conditions are now manifest. A hopeless struggle for sovereignty has degenerated into a strife which means not the useless, but the wanton sacrifice of human life, and the utter destruction of the subject-matter of the conflict.

What further manifestations are needed? Is it that the American people doubt the sources from which their information comes? They are the consuls all over the island of Cuba. For what voice crying in the wilderness are they still waiting? What will convince them that the time has come?

If the United States is to interfere in this matter she should do so at once, but she should only
do so after she has informed herself thoroughly
concerning it. She should not act on the reports
of the hotel piazza correspondents, but send men
to Cuba on whose judgment and common sense she
can rely. General Fitzhugh Lee is one of these
men, and there is no better informed American on
Cuban matters than he, nor one who sees more
clearly the course which our government should
pursue. Through the consuls all over the island,
he is in touch with every part of it, and in daily
touch; but incidents which are frightfully true there
seem exaggerated and overdrawn when a typewrit-
ten description of them reaches the calm corridors
of the State Department.

More men like Lee should go to Cuba to inform
themselves, not men who will stop in Havana and
pick up the gossip of the Hotel Ingleterra, but who
will go out into the cities and sugar plantations and
talk to the consuls and merchants and planters,
both Spanish and American; who can see for themselves the houses burning and the smoke arising
from every point of the landscape; who can see the
bodies of "pacificos" brought into the cities, and
who can sit on a porch of an American planter's
house and hear him tell in a whisper how his sugar

cane was set on fire by the same Spanish soldiers who surround the house, and who are supposed to guard his property, but who, in reality, are there to keep a watch on him.

He should hear little children, born of American parents, come into the consulate and ask for a piece of bread. He should see the children and the women herded in the towns or walking the streets in long processions, with the Mayor at their head, begging his fellow Spaniards to give them food, the children covered with the red blotches of small-pox and the women gaunt with yellow fever. He should see hundreds of thousands of dollars' worth of machinery standing idle, covered with rust and dirt, or lying twisted and broken under fallen walls. He will learn that while one hundred and fifty-six vessels came into the port of Matanzas in 1894, only eighty-eight came in 1895, and that but sixteen touched there in 1896, and that while the export of sugar from that port to the United States in 1894 amounted to eleven millions of dollars, in 1895 it sank to eight millions of dollars, and in 1896 it did not reach one million.   I copied these figures one morning from the consular books, and that loss of ten millions of dollars in two years in one little port is but a sample of the facts that show what chaos this war is working.

Spanish Cavalryman on a Texas Broncho

In three weeks any member of the Senate or of Congress who wishes to inform himself on this reign of terror in Cuba can travel from one end of this island to the other and return competent to speak with absolute authority. No man, no matter what his prejudices may be, can make this journey and not go home convinced that it is his duty to try to stop this cruel waste of life and this wanton destruction of a beautiful country.

A reign of terror sounds hysterical, but it is an exact and truthful descriptive phrase of the condition in Cuba. Insurgents and Spaniards alike are laying waste the land, and neither side shows any sign of giving up the struggle. But while the men are in the field fighting after their fashion, for the independence of the island, the old men and the infirm and the women and children, who cannot help the cause or themselves, and who are destitute and starving and dying, have their eyes turned toward the great republic that lies only eighty miles away, and they are holding out their hands and asking "How long, O, Lord, how long?"

Or if the members of the Senate and of Congress can not visit Cuba, why will they not listen to those who have been there? Of three men who traveled over the island, seeking the facts concerning it, two correspondents and an interpreter, two of the three were for a time in Spanish hospitals, covered with small-pox. Of the three, although we were together until they were taken ill, I was the only one who escaped contagion.

If these other men should die, they die because they tried to find out the truth. Is it likely, having risked such a price for it that they would lie about what they have seen?

They could have invented stories of famine and disease in Havana. They need not have looked for the facts where they were to be found, in the seaports and villages and fever camps. Why not listen to these men or to Stephen Bonsal, of the *New York Herald,* in whom the late President showed his confidence by appointing him to two diplomatic missions?

Why not listen to C. E. Akers, of the *London Times,* and *Harper's Weekly,* who has held two commissions from the Queen? Why disregard a dozen other correspondents who are seeking the truth, and who urge in every letter which they write that their country should stop this destruction of a beautiful land and this butchery of harmless non-combatants?

The matter lies at the door of Congress. Each day's delay means the death of hundreds of people, every hour sees fresh blood spilled, and

For Cuba Libre

more houses and more acres of crops sinking into ashes. A month's delay means the loss to this world of thousands of lives, the unchecked growth of terrible diseases, and the spreading devastation of a great plague.

It would be an insult to urge political reasons, or the sure approval of the American people which the act of interference would bring, or any other unworthy motive. No European power dare interfere, and it lies with the United States and with her people to give the signal. If it is given now it will save thousands of innocent lives; if it is delayed just that many people will perish.

THE END.